REGIONS OF THE UNITED STATES
EXPLORE THE
SOUTH

by Kristine Spanier, MLIS

pogo

Ideas for Parents and Teachers

Pogo Books let children practice reading informational text while introducing them to nonfiction features such as headings, labels, sidebars, maps, and diagrams, as well as a table of contents, glossary, and index.

Carefully leveled text with a strong photo match offers early fluent readers the support they need to succeed.

Before Reading

- "Walk" through the book and point out the various nonfiction features. Ask the student what purpose each feature serves.
- Look at the glossary together. Read and discuss the words.

Read the Book

- Have the child read the book independently.
- Invite him or her to list questions that arise from reading.

After Reading

- Discuss the child's questions. Talk about how he or she might find answers to those questions.
- Prompt the child to think more. Ask: The Civil Rights Movement started in the South. Did you know about this movement before you read this book? What more would you like to learn about it?

Pogo Books are published by Jump!
5357 Penn Avenue South
Minneapolis, MN 55419
www.jumplibrary.com

Copyright © 2023 Jump!
International copyright reserved in all countries.
No part of this book may be reproduced in any form without written permission from the publisher.

Library of Congress Cataloging-in-Publication Data

Names: Spanier, Kristine, author.
Title: Explore the South / by Kristine Spanier, MLIS.
Description: Minneapolis, MN: Jump!, Inc., [2023].
Series: Regions of the United States
Includes index. | Audience: Ages 7-10
Identifiers: LCCN 2021055758 (print)
LCCN 2021055759 (ebook)
ISBN 9781636907239 (hardcover)
ISBN 9781636907246 (paperback)
ISBN 9781636907253 (ebook)
Subjects: LCSH: Southern States—Juvenile literature.
Classification: LCC F209.3 .S687 2023 (print)
LCC F209.3 (ebook) | DDC 975—dc23/eng/20211209
LC record available at https://lccn.loc.gov/2021055758
LC ebook record available at https://lccn.loc.gov/2021055759

Editor: Jenna Gleisner
Designer: Molly Ballanger

Photo Credits: Kevin Ruck/Shutterstock, cover (left), 22t; Mooneydriver/iStock, cover (right); Stacy Funderburke/Shutterstock, cover (bottom); Irina Wilhauk/Shutterstock, 1; Andrea Izzotti/Shutterstock, 3; dszc/iStock, 4; Album/sfgp/SuperStock, 5; George A. Kenna/Shutterstock, 6-7; Image Barbara Cushing/Everett Collection/SuperStock, 8-9; Joe Pearl Photography/iStock, 10; marineke thissen/Shutterstock, 11; KenCanning/iStock, 12-13; Mark Conlin/Alamy, 14-15tl; Gary Rolband/Shutterstock, 14-15tr; NajaShots/iStock, 14-15bl; SannaBlue/Shutterstock, 14-15br; Walter Arce/Dreamstime, 16; Erika Goldring/Getty, 17; Art Wager/iStock, 18-19; Hollie Davenport/EyeEm/Getty, 20-21; ABDESIGN/iStock, 22m; Joanne Dale/Shutterstock, 22b; Wangkun Jia/Shutterstock, 23.

Printed in the United States of America at Corporate Graphics in North Mankato, Minnesota.

Title Page Image: Everglades National Park, Florida

TABLE OF CONTENTS

CHAPTER 1
History and Location.........................4

CHAPTER 2
Geography and Wildlife...................10

CHAPTER 3
Daily Life...................................16

QUICK FACTS & TOOLS
Quick Facts.................................22
Glossary....................................23
Index.......................................24
To Learn More.............................24

CHAPTER 1

HISTORY AND LOCATION

In the early 1800s, **settlers** in the United States began moving south. They wanted to grow crops year-round in the warm **climate**. **Indigenous** people lived on the land. The government forced them to leave.

cotton field

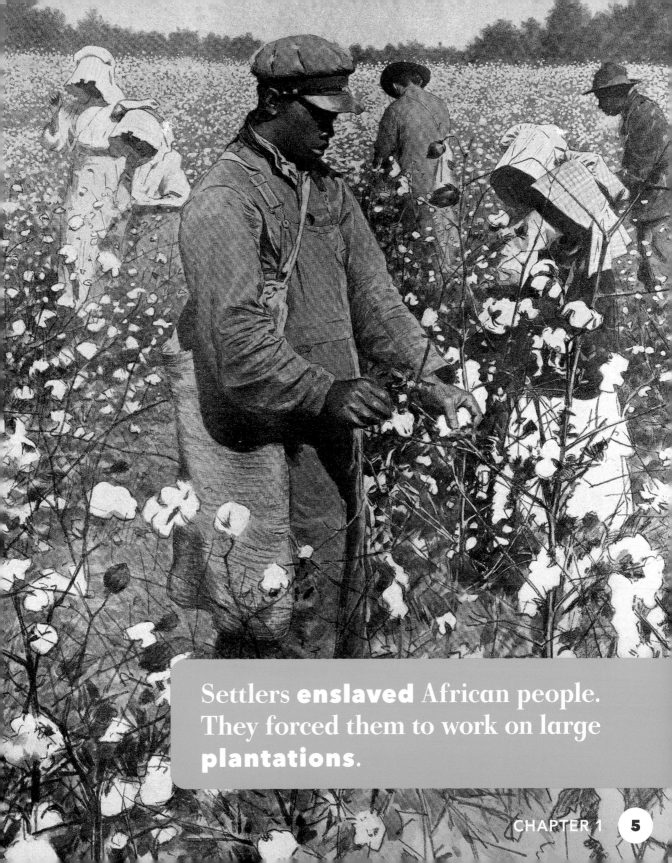

Settlers **enslaved** African people. They forced them to work on large **plantations**.

Many people in northern states wanted to end **slavery**. Many people in the South **Region** did not. The Civil War (1861–1865) broke out. It started at Fort Sumter in South Carolina. The South eventually lost the war. Slavery came to an end.

Fort Sumter

TAKE A LOOK!

Ten states make up the South. Take a look!

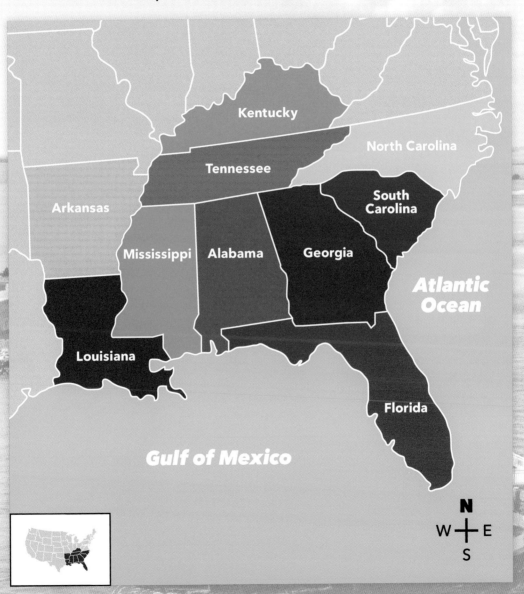

Kentucky

North Carolina

Tennessee

Arkansas

South Carolina

Mississippi   Alabama   Georgia

Atlantic Ocean

Louisiana

Florida

Gulf of Mexico

N
W — E
S

The **Civil Rights** Movement began in the South. In 1955, Rosa Parks was riding a bus in Montgomery, Alabama. The bus driver told her to give her seat to a white person. She said no. As a result, she was arrested. People stopped riding the buses. They spoke out against **segregation**.

WHAT DO YOU THINK?

In 1965, Martin Luther King Jr. organized peaceful marches in Alabama. Marchers wanted equal voting rights for Black people. President Lyndon Johnson signed the Voting Rights **Act** of 1965. This made it easier for Black people to vote. Why is it important everyone is able to vote?

Rosa Parks • • • • •▸

CHAPTER 2

GEOGRAPHY AND WILDLIFE

The South is filled with interesting things to see. Alligators live in many of the southern states. Louisiana and Florida have the highest **populations** of them.

alligator

Okefenokee **Swamp** is in Georgia. It is the largest swamp in North America. Some plants here are meat-eaters. Pitcher plants are one kind. They catch and eat insects and spiders.

pitcher plant

Great Smoky Mountains

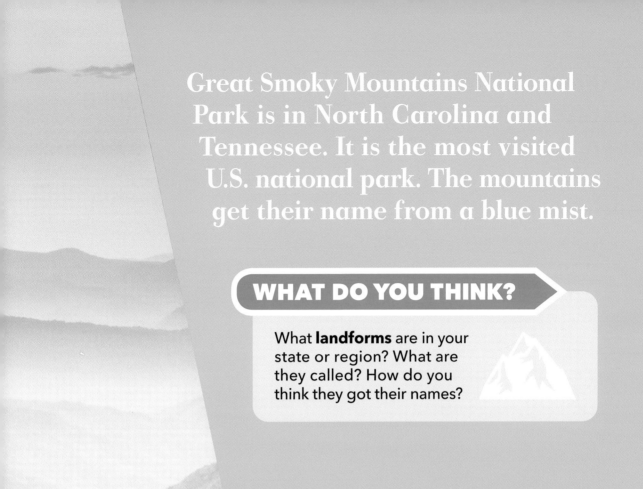

Great Smoky Mountains National Park is in North Carolina and Tennessee. It is the most visited U.S. national park. The mountains get their name from a blue mist.

WHAT DO YOU THINK?

What **landforms** are in your state or region? What are they called? How do you think they got their names?

Florida panthers prowl the forests. Wild boars look for food. Diamondback rattlesnakes slither. Wild turkeys walk, run, and fly through the South!

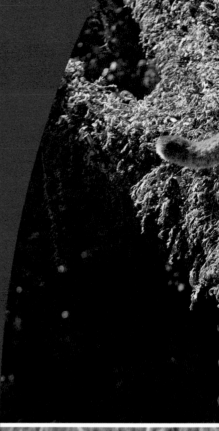

Florida panther

wild boar

diamondback rattlesnake

wild turkey

CHAPTER 3

DAILY LIFE

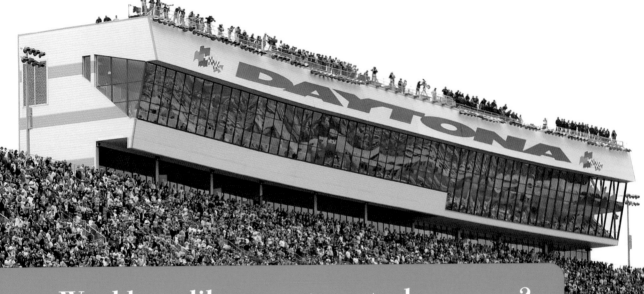

Would you like to go to a stock car race? You'll find many racetracks in the South. The Daytona 500 is in Florida. This race is 500 miles (805 kilometers) long!

Mardi Gras is a celebration. It takes place every year in New Orleans, Louisiana. People dance and watch parades. They eat purple, yellow, and green cakes.

cargo ship

Farming is important in the South. Astronauts work at the John F. Kennedy Space Center in Florida. **Cargo** ships move in and out of Louisiana's **ports**. They travel through the Gulf of Mexico. They go all over the world from here!

TAKE A LOOK!

What are some of the South's top **industries**? Take a look!

Alabama

Arkansas

Florida

Georgia

Kentucky

Louisiana

Mississippi

North Carolina

South Carolina

Tennessee

 = aerospace   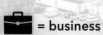 = business    = farming   = fishing

 = food processing   = iron, steel, and oil production   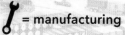 = manufacturing

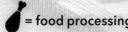 = maritime transport   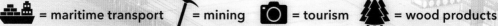 = mining   = tourism    = wood products

Myrtle Beach,
South Carolina

The South is usually warm all year. Summers are hot. People go to the beach. Winters are mild, but you can still find snow in the mountains!

There is a lot to explore in the South. What would you like to see first?

SOUTH REGION

NASHVILLE, TN

Location: southeastern United States

Population (2021 estimate): 75,446,953

Most Populated City in Each State:
Huntsville, AL
Little Rock, AR
Jacksonville, FL
Atlanta, GA
Louisville, KY
New Orleans, LA
Jackson, MS
Charlotte, NC
Charleston, SC
Nashville, TN

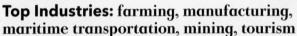
OZARK MOUNTAINS, AR

Top Industries: farming, manufacturing, maritime transportation, mining, tourism

Average High Temperature:
90 degrees Fahrenheit (32 degrees Celsius)

Average Low Temperature:
35 degrees Fahrenheit (2 degrees Celsius)

OKEFENOKEE SWAMP, GA

Major Landforms: Appalachian Mountains, Ozark Mountains, Ouachita Mountains, Great Smoky Mountains

Highest Point: Mount Mitchell, NC, 6,684 feet (2,037 m)

Major Waterways: Mississippi River, Arkansas River, Red River, Ohio River, Lake Okeechobee, Lake Pontchartrain, Gulf of Mexico, Okefenokee Swamp

Major Landmarks: Everglades National Park, Great Smoky Mountains National Park, John F. Kennedy Space Center, Fort Sumter

GLOSSARY

act: A bill that has been passed by Congress. If signed by the president, it becomes law.

cargo: Goods that are carried by a ship, plane, train, truck, or other vehicle.

civil rights: The individual rights that all members of a democratic society have to freedom and equal treatment under the law.

climate: The weather typical of a certain place over a long period of time.

enslaved: Owned by another and treated as property.

Indigenous: Of or relating to the earliest known people to live in a place.

industries: Businesses or trades.

landforms: Natural features of land surfaces.

plantations: Large farms found in warm climates.

populations: The total numbers of people or creatures who live in certain places.

ports: Towns or cities with harbors where ships can load and unload goods.

region: A general area or a specific district or territory.

segregation: The act or practice of keeping people or groups apart from a main group.

settlers: People who make a home or live in a new place.

slavery: A system in which people owned other people and treated them as property.

swamp: An area of wet, spongy ground.

INDEX

African people 5

Alabama 7, 8, 19

Arkansas 7, 19

Atlantic Ocean 7, 14

Civil Rights Movement 8

Civil War 6

climate 4, 21

Daytona 500 16

Florida 7, 10, 14, 16, 18, 19

Fort Sumter 6

Georgia 7, 11, 19

Great Smoky Mountains National Park 13

Gulf of Mexico 7, 18

Indigenous people 4

industries 18, 19

John F. Kennedy Space Center 18

Kentucky 7, 19

Louisiana 7, 10, 17, 18, 19

Mardi Gras 17

Mississippi 7, 19

New Orleans, Louisiana 17

North Carolina 7, 13, 19

Okefenokee Swamp 11

plantations 5

South Carolina 6, 7, 19

Tennessee 7, 13, 19

wildlife 10, 11, 14

TO LEARN MORE

Finding more information is as easy as 1, 2, 3.

❶ Go to www.factsurfer.com

❷ Enter "exploretheSouth" into the search box.

❸ Choose your book to see a list of websites.

FACT SURFER